CLASSIC ROCK FOR CELLO

Audio Access Included

Visit **www.halleonard.com/mylibrary**

Enter Code

7610-4767-6796-0367

D0613724

Audio Arrangements by Peter Deneff
Tracking, mixing, and mastering by BeatHouse Music

ISBN 978-1-4803-5455-5

HAL•LEONARD®
CORPORATION

7777 W. BLUEMOUND RD. P.O. BOX 13819 MILWAUKEE, WI 53213

Visit Hal Leonard Online at
www.halleonard.com

CONTENTS

4 Another One Bites the Dust
Queen

5 Born to Be Wild
Steppenwolf

6 Brown Eyed Girl
Van Morrison

8 Dust in the Wind
Kansas

7 Every Breath You Take
Sting

8 Fly Like an Eagle
Steve Miller Band

10 I Heard It Through the Grapevine
Marvin Gaye

11 I Shot the Sheriff
Eric Clapton

12 Oye Como Va
Santana

9 Up Around the Bend
Creedence Clearwater Revival

ANOTHER ONE BITES THE DUST

Words and Music by
JOHN DEACON

Steady Rock

BORN TO BE WILD

Words and Music by
MARS BONFIRE

BROWN EYED GIRL

Words and Music by
VAN MORRISON

EVERY BREATH YOU TAKE

Words and Music by
STING

DUST IN THE WIND

Words and Music by
KERRY LIVGREN

FLY LIKE AN EAGLE

Words and Music by
STEVE MILLER

UP AROUND THE BEND

Words and Music by
JOHN FOGERTY

I HEARD IT THROUGH THE GRAPEVINE

Words and Music by NORMAN J. WHITFIELD
amd BARRETT STRONG

I SHOT THE SHERIFF

Words and Music by
BOB MARLEY

OYE COMO VA

Words and Music by
TITO PUENTE

Moderate Latin Rock